ADVENTURE TIME: BRAIN ROBBERS
ISBN - 978-1-78585-9-267

Published by Titan Comics, a division of Titan Publishing Group Ltd., 144 Southwark St., London, SE1 0UP. ADVENTURE TIME, CARTOON NETWORK, the logos, and all related characters and elements are trademarks of and © Cartoon Network. (S16) All rights reserved. All characters, events and institutions depicted herein are fictional. Any similarity between any of the names, characters, persons, events and/or institutions in this publication to actual names, characters, and persons, whether living or dead and/or institutions are unintended and purely coincidental.

A CIP catalogue record for this title is available from the British Library.

Printed in China.

10 9 8 7 6 5 4 3 2 1

Created by Pendleton Ward

Written by **Josh Trujillo**

Pencils by **Zachary Sterling**

Inks by **Jenna Ayoub & Phil Murphy**

Colours by **Joie Foster**
with **Laura Langston**

Letters by **Warren Montgomery**

Cover by **Scott Maynard**

With Special Thanks to Marisa Marionakis, Janet No, Curtis Lelash, Conrad Montgomery, Meghan Bradley, Kelly Crews, Scott Malchus, Adam Muto and the wonderful folks at Cartoon Network.

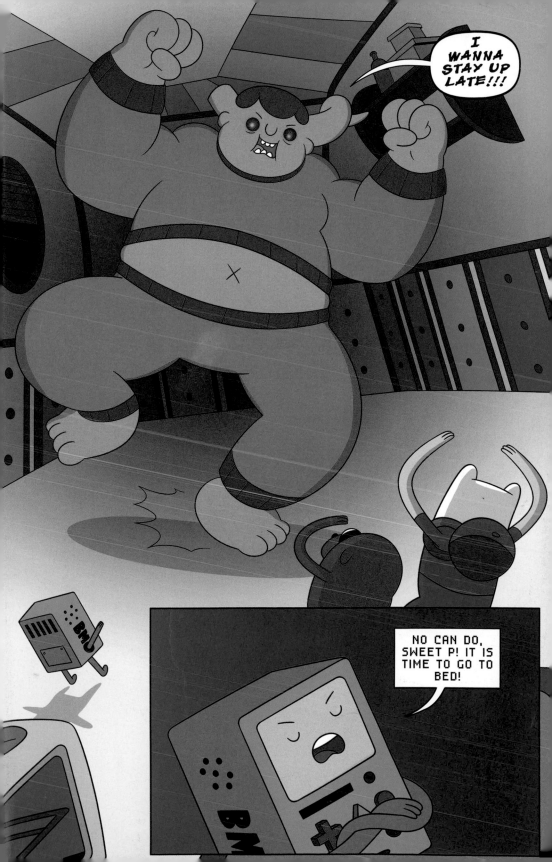

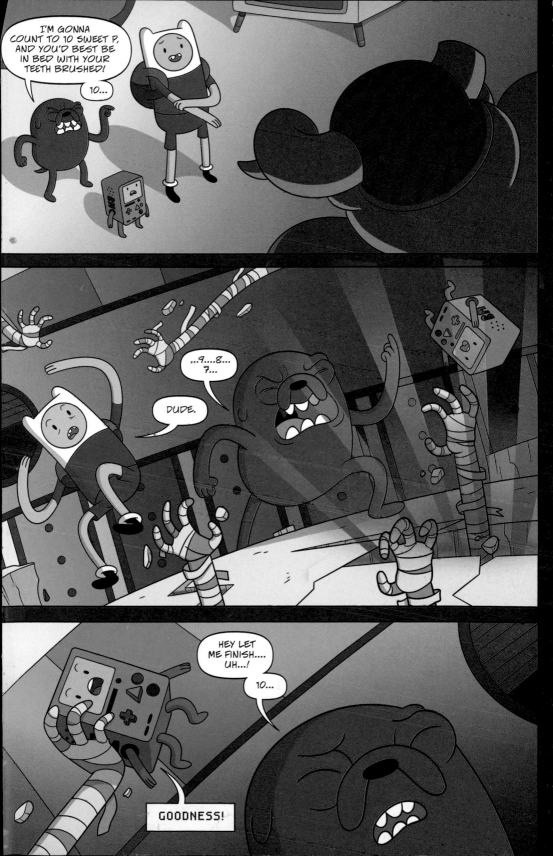

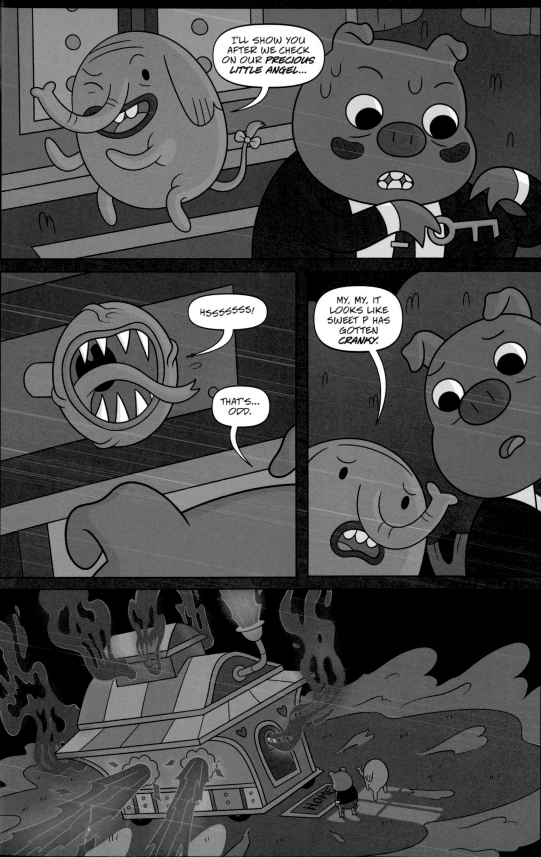

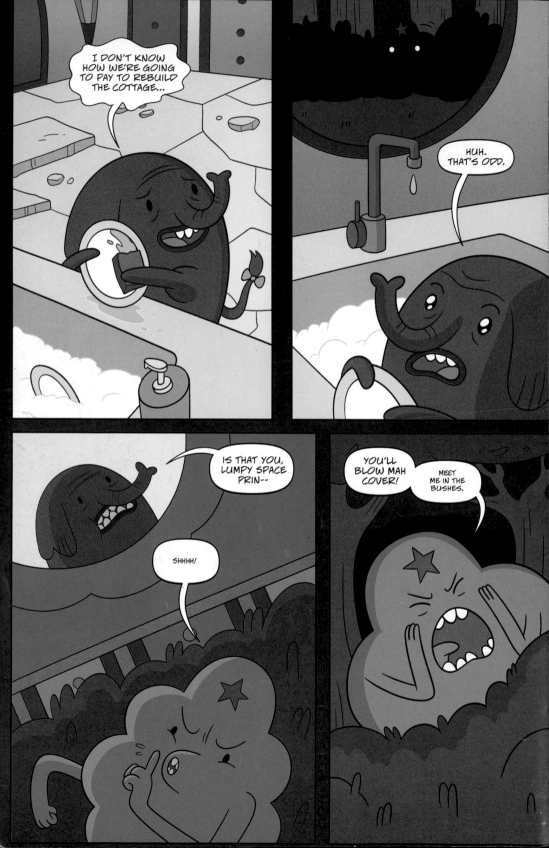

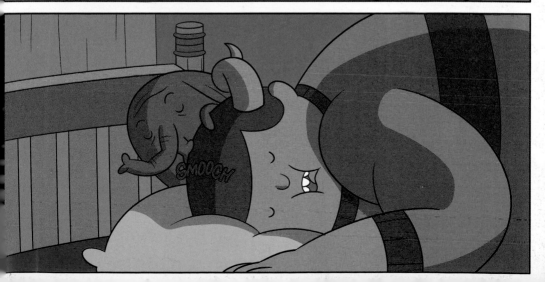

SMOOCH

WHOOAAAA!!

THEY ARE GETTING AWAY!

WHAT?!

SORRY, I WAS LOOKING AT THESE CLOUDS.

PRETTY, PRETTY CLOUDS.

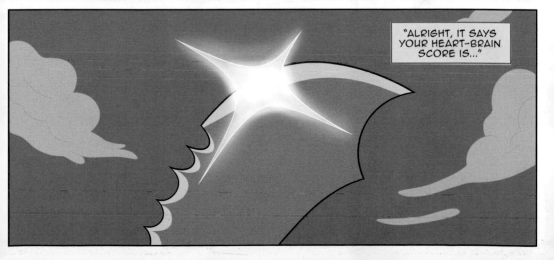

BRRROUUUGN?

HISSSS...

SPRACK!

SPOUCK

SPUT

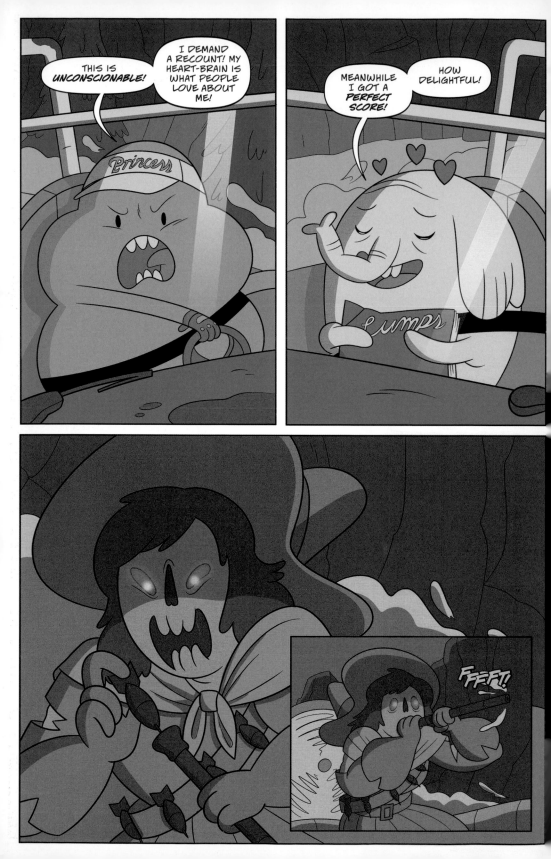

MY NAME IS TREE TRUNKS AND THIS IS MY ADVENTURE BUDDY, LUMPY SPACE PRINCESS!

TREE TRUNKS!? IT'S ME-- GUTTERKISSER!

YOU USED TO COME HERE ALL THE TIME!

GUTTERKISSER! I REMEMBER YOU! HOW HAVE YOU BEEN?

NOT BAD!

I'M DEAD NOW!

WE'RE ON A THRILLING MISSION TO FIND A LOST FORTUNE, BUT OUR DUNE BUGGY GOT EATEN!

MAYBE THE BOSS'LL HELP YOU.

BOSS, EH?

LONG TIME, NO SEE...LSP.

GUILDMASTER!

I ASSUME YOU'RE HERE TO APOLOGIZE.

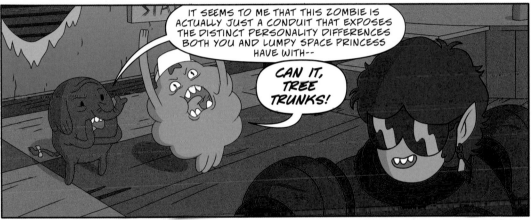

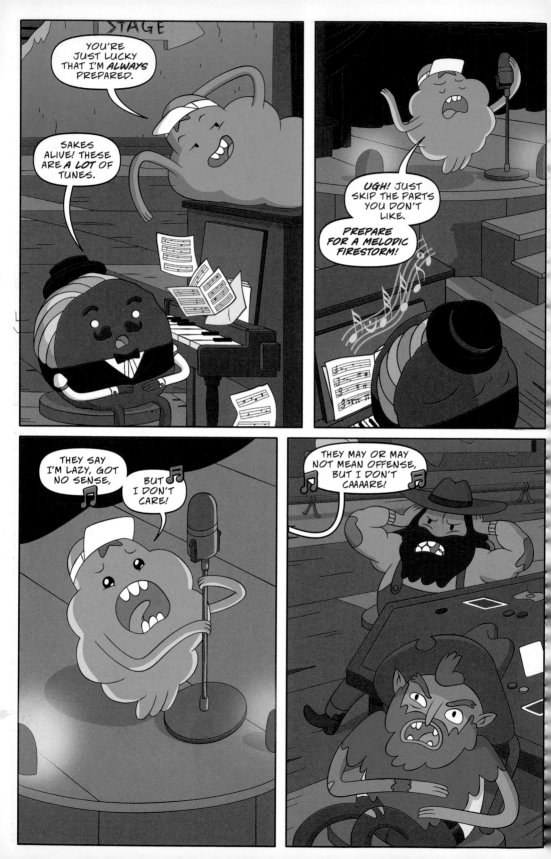

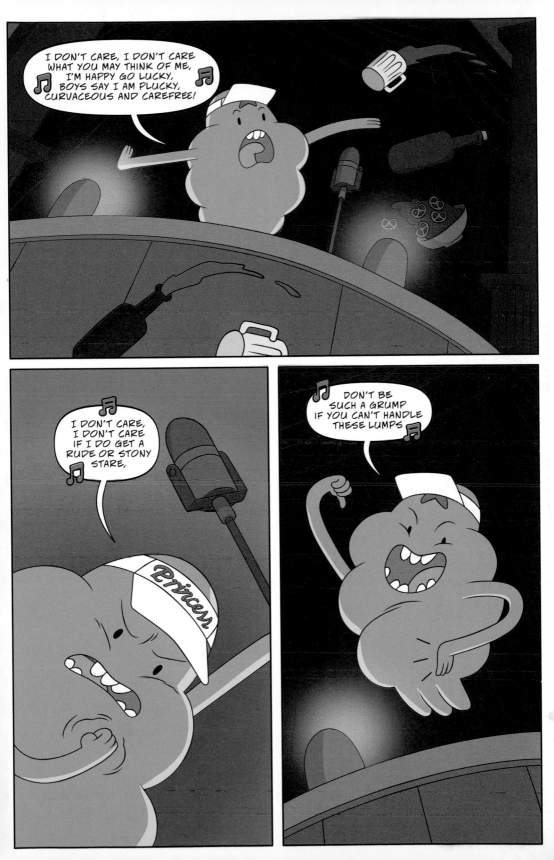

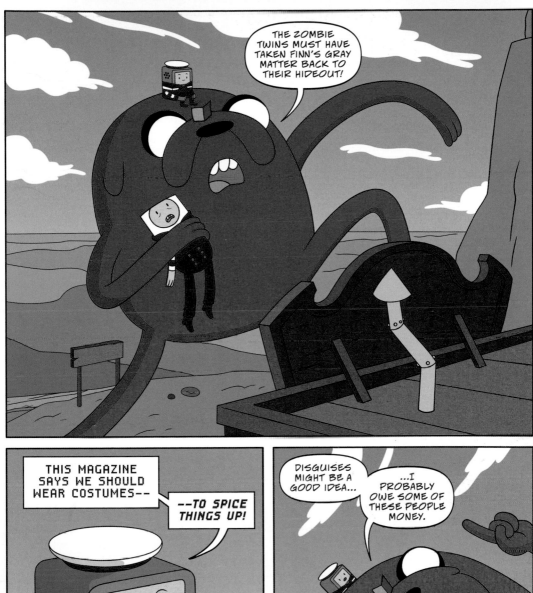

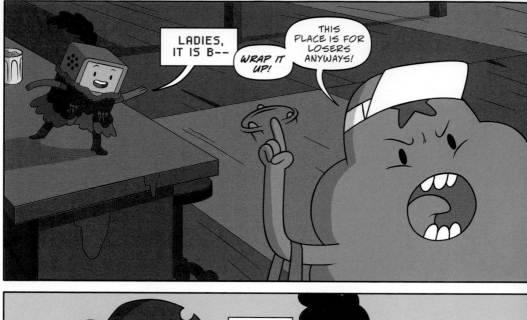

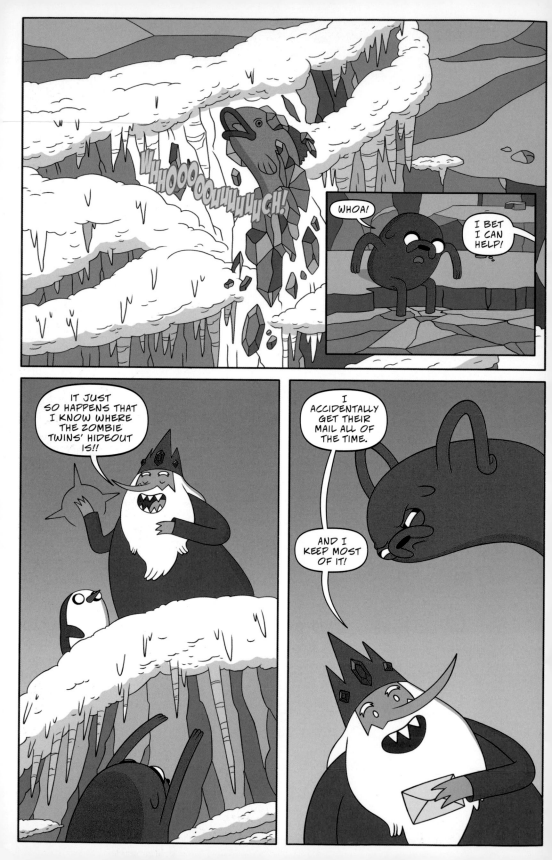

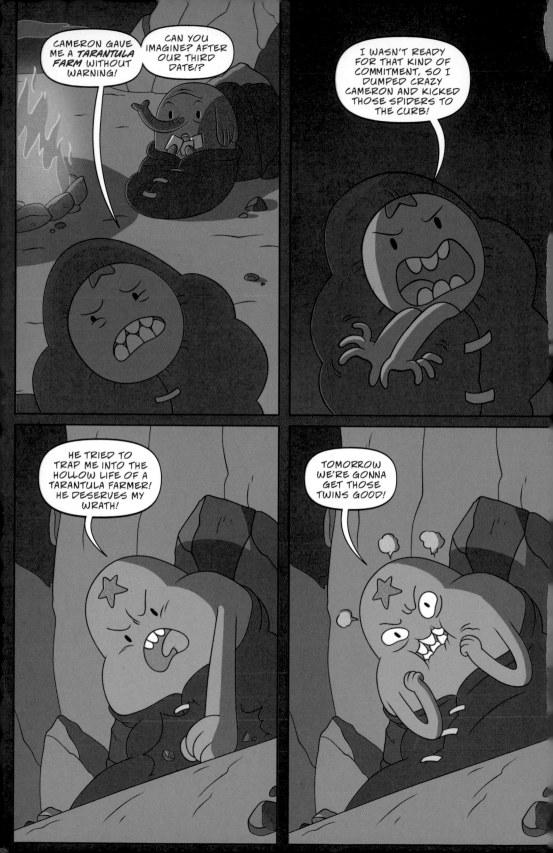

WAZZAAAA?

THIS DOESN'T LOOK RIGHT!

WE MADE IT, PAL!

THIS PLACE IS THE BEST BRUNCH SPOT IN OOO, AT LEAST AFTER BREAKFAST PRINCESS UPPED HER SECURITY DETAIL!

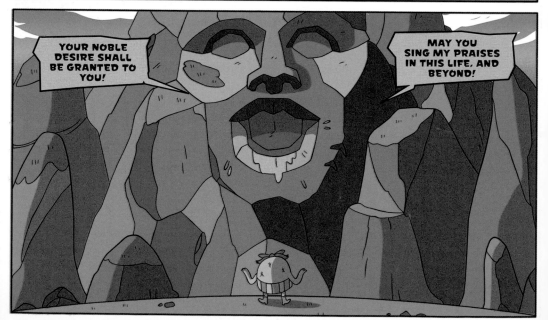

WOW! THANKS!

NOBODY SAID ANYTHING ABOUT BRUNCH!

BUT IT'S BRUNCH TIME!

LOOK "ICE FRIEND," I'M STARTING TO WORRY ABOUT FINN.

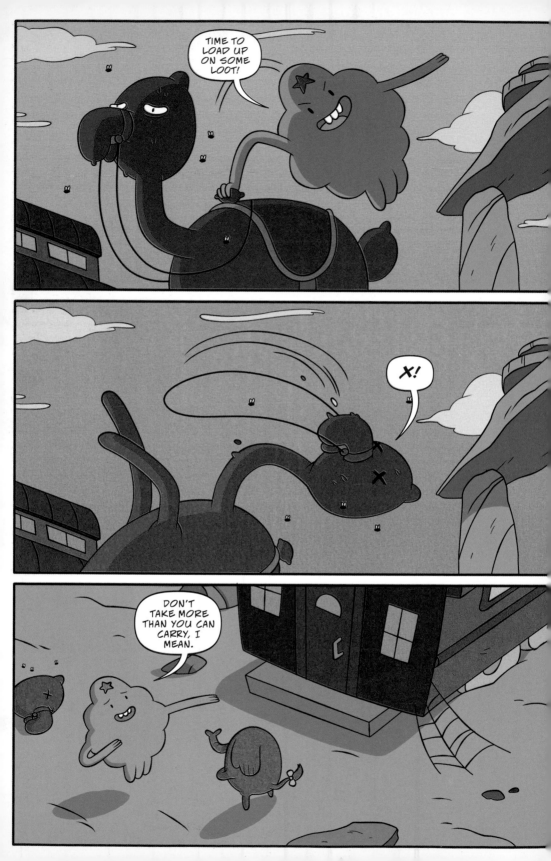

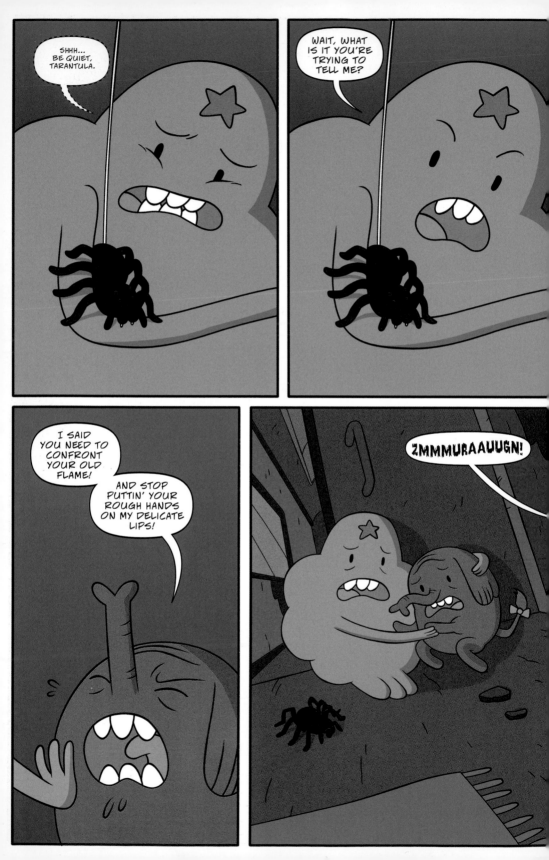

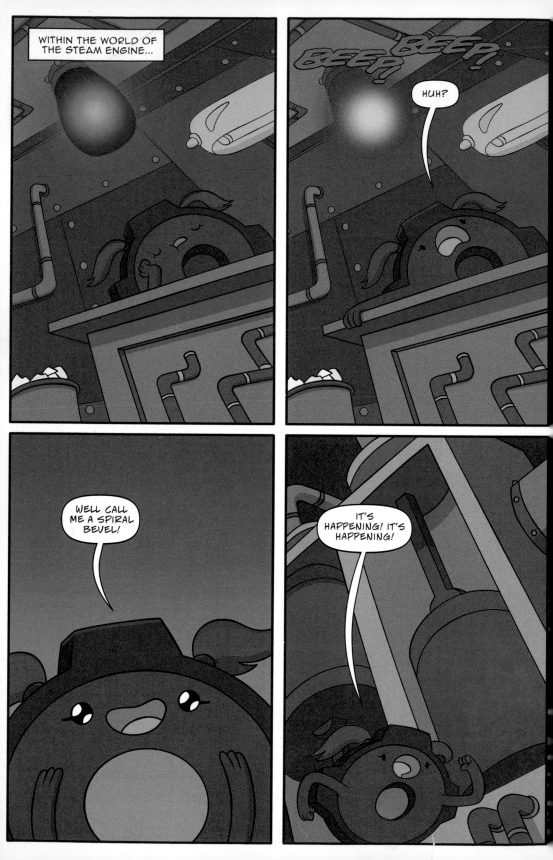

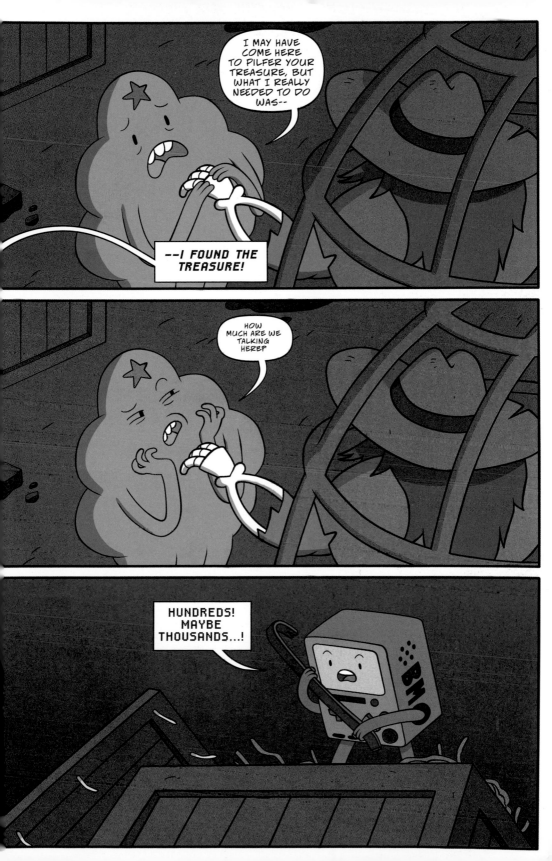

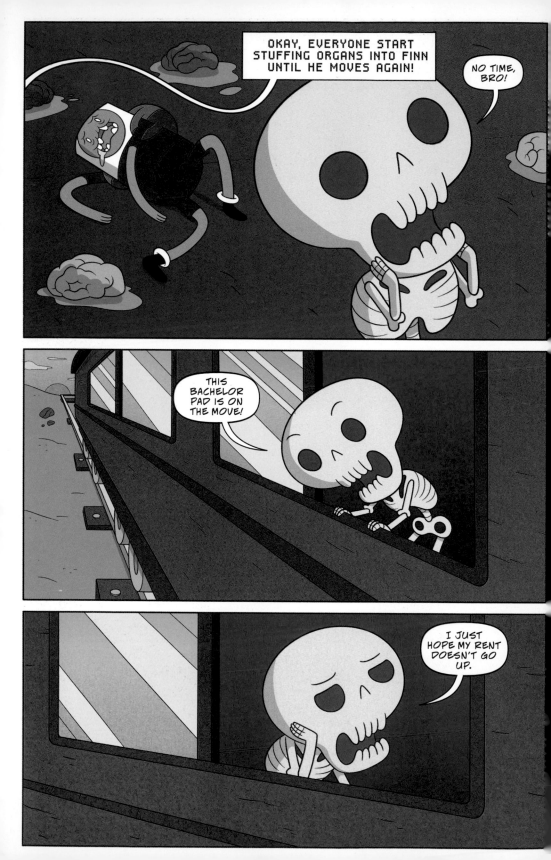

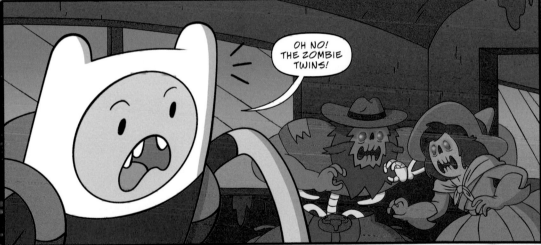

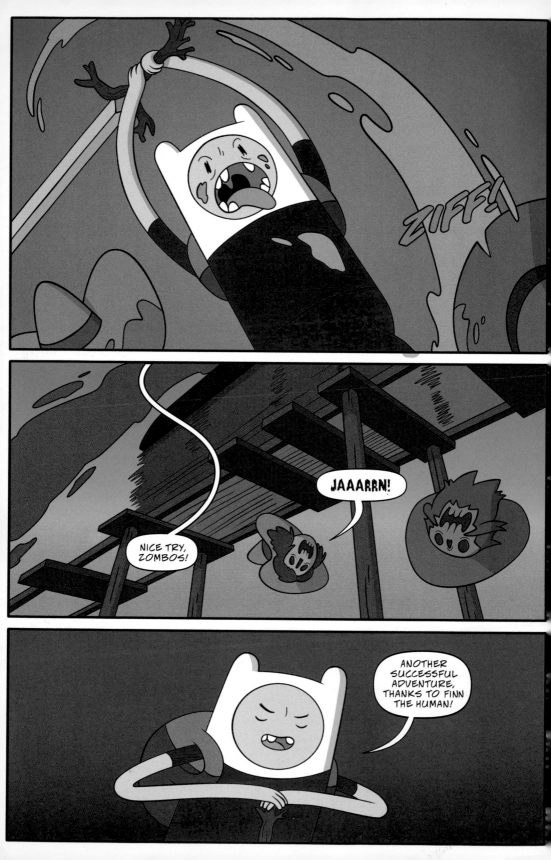

"FOR ALL OF OUR FRIENDS!"

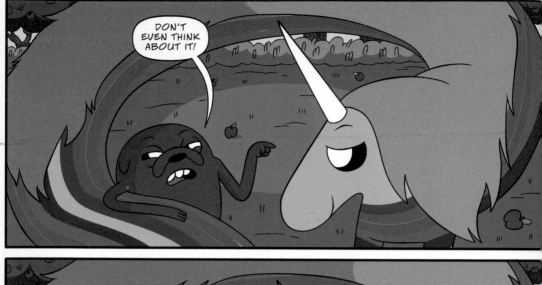

WE'RE EATING BRAINS?!

BWAAAK

MY SWEET P IS A GROWING BOY. I WASN'T ABOUT TO LET THEM GO TO WASTE!

PLUS I HAD A GOOD RECIPE.

DELISH!

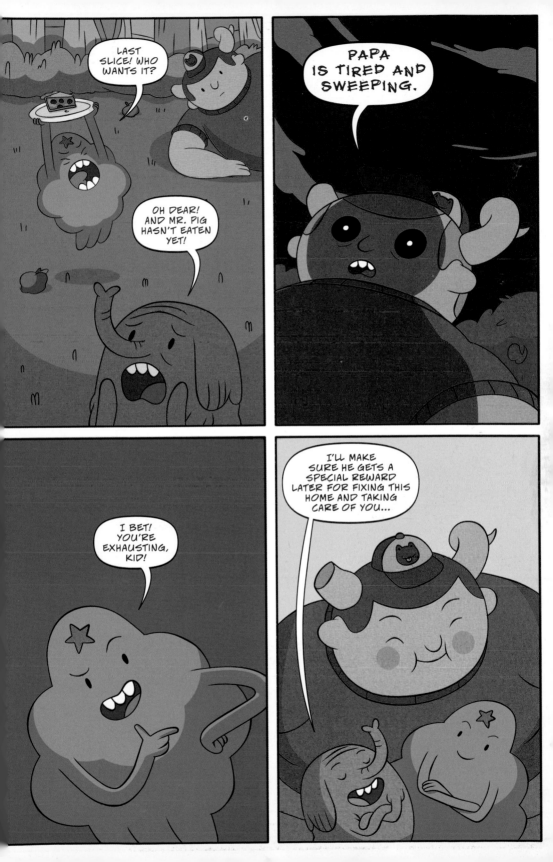